PONY TALES 2

More Memories of Abingdon RDA
- 50th Anniversary Edition

Edited by Angy Irvin
& Illustrated by
Amanda Graham

CONTENTS

Title Page
FOREWORD   1
A LIFE CHANGING SURPRISE   4
THE JOY OF TEAMWORK   10
MY EXPERIENCE OF RIDING A HORSE   12
HIGHLIGHTS OF ABINGDON GROUP TAKEN FROM THE MINUTES 1975 - 1995 14
NEVER WORK WITH CHILDREN OR ANIMALS…   20
RDA STORY   23
RIDING   26
RDA AND WHAT IT MEANS TO US   28
CANTER ON MR B   31
LOVELY LISA   32
PURPOSE IN LIFE   33
THE FUNDAY AND I CAME FOURTH!   35
THE ADVENTURES OF HARRY AND   38

MARSHALL	
BINGO IN THE BARLOW ARENA	43
RIDGEWAY MEMORIES	46
BRYN – ANGEL OR DEVIL?	48
RDA AND ME	52
ABINGDON RIDING FOR THE DISABLED	54
MY DRAWING	56
CHEEKY JASPER	57
MY STORY	59
SOME LESSONS ARE MORE EVENTFUL THAN OTHERS!	61
ME AND RANGER	66
A LETTER TO BRYN	70
RIDING	73
BRAVE ROSIE	75
WASHING BRYN	78
RIDER AND PARENT'S VIEWS	80
MY RDA STORY	82
MINTY SMELL	84
WALKING ON MY OWN	85
THANK YOU RDA ABINGDON!	87
REMEMBERING LILY	89
MAPLE AND MARSHALL'S ADVENTURE	92
SHUSH!	97
THUNDER AND LIGHTNING	100

THOUGHTS FROM IRIS AND THE BUNCE FAMILY	102
NEARLY 50 YEARS	105
MY LOVE OF RIDING	108
MR BROWN	110
SENSATIONAL HELPERS	112
VOLUNTEERING	115
WHEN SANTA CAME TO THE PARTY…	116
MAKING A DIFFERENCE	119
VOLUNTEERING	122
MY RDA STORY	124
BRILLIANT BRYN	128
WHEN THE UKULELE PLAYERS CAME TO TOWN	130
MY LIFE WITH RDA - SO FAR!	133
A ROYAL VISIT	136
THE NEW ARENA	139
ALESSIA'S STORY	142
BRYN'S SORE TEETH	145
MY DRAWING OF BRYN	149
THANK YOU	150
Acknowledgement	155

FOREWORD

By Angy Irvin

This year 2025 marks a landmark birthday for Abingdon Group RDA and I wanted to help celebrate by producing this book. It is a collection of memories and stories from riders, parents, coaches, helpers, fundraisers and other volunteers.

Having recently had my own landmark birthday (yes, I'm approximately a year older than Abingdon RDA) has made me reflect on my life and what a big part of it Abingdon RDA has been and continues to be. As I've got older I've realised that very few people do anything world-changingly big in their lives such as invent penicillin or design London Bridge, but lots of people can make a difference in lots of ways. This book is full of examples of people making a big difference in a little way.

A massive thank you to all who contributed to this book; the ponies and riders who feature in the stories; everyone who contributed a story; Ruth Gerring for her wonderful drawings; the photographers; Lesley Chaundy for proof-reading; Val Evans of Val Evans Designs for the brilliant cover design and lastly (but definitely not least) Amanda Graham for her amazing illustrations, proof-reading, photography and unwavering support, advice and ideas.

This is dedicated to everyone (human and equine) who is or has been part of Abingdon RDA in the last 50 years – here's to the next 50!!

A LIFE CHANGING SURPRISE

by Sam Davies

On a sunny Saturday morning way back in 1985, 4 year old me was plonked in the back of the car and told the destination would be a surprise.

A bit miffed and bored, I decided to take a nap. I'm not a nice person when awoken from my slumber, especially not when all I've been woken for is an old caravan in the middle of a farm!! And in this caravan they want to put a helmet on my head??!!! A helmet that me and my head, have no want or need for thank you very much, just let me sleep on my Dad's shoulder. Some surprise this was turning out to be!

Then we were out of the caravan, me unfortunately with that stupid thing on my head, and over to the indoor arena....

Horses!!!!

I've got the helmet on my head because I'm going to ride a horse?

Me???

On that beast there??!!

No chance, ain't happening, didn't even want the helmet in the first place, remember?

Then I was grudgingly introduced to Drago. The grandad of all the horses. The safest, most reliable of them all, and half asleep just like me! When it was pointed out that he was shaped like a rather comfy armchair, I plucked up the courage to give it a go. He was way comfier than any armchair ever!! I lent down to give him a pat on his warm soft neck, and his withers tickled my nose. That was me done, I was in love.

Saturday mornings couldn't come around quick enough. That old caravan became my happy place, I couldn't wait to get in there, put a helmet on my head and look in the book to see who I would be riding. I loved all the horses like they were my own. From Drago, to Sophie who always had a spring in her step, Rondo (I know any of you reading this, that knew Rondo, just let out a little happy sigh when you read his name) who was just amazing at everything, and I mean everything! There wasn't enough of him to go around at dressage time. Then there was Tufty who always looked like she'd had a rough night. Sweet Jayjay who would take a polo from my lips and Garva who would take off pretty much anytime he was bored, more often than not with the unlucky James on his back.

During the week, I'd have to make do with tying a rope around my tricycle to lead/drag it round the garden. I'd also pray every night for a Shetland pony (no way would my mum let me keep a full-size horse!). If I could have run away from home to live at the stables, I'd have been on it and my life would have been complete (this still stands now, if I disappear please don't tell my kids where I am).

It wasn't just the horses either. I fell in love with all the instructors, helpers and riders too.

We all had so much fun. Every lesson was full of giggles, camaraderie and joy. Once we had our very own stables and arena built the adventures really began. Riding the horses to the local pub one sunny evening, playing hide and seek on horseback behind the enormous hay bales in the farmer's field. And of course the sponsored ride!

Princess Anne officially opening our new stables was a biggie. As part of the display we performed for the opening, it was my job to attach bells on both the hind legs of Rondo (sigh!) We lined up to meet Princess Anne after, and when it was my turn, she pointed out to me that I had a ladybird on my jumper! I was so chuffed, until I saw the staggering amount of meringues at the buffet, now that was something to be chuffed about!

Together, we endured the musical ride we performed to "The Teddy Bears Picnic" one year. We practised that delight a million times (I'm not exaggerating) and we still somehow managed to muck it up when it came to performance time!

The gymkhana games at the regionals, up against the other RDA crews, brought out a side to our helpers that we hadn't seen before. This was serious business; we were not losing. Helper either side, demon runner (I won't name names, you know who you are) leading Rondo (see, good for everything!) I was told, just hold on!!!! We were on fire, so much so Rondo broke into a canter and we had to turn a penalty circle, meaning we lost the race. I was glad I'd managed to just hold on!

My favourite of all our adventures, was taking the horses up to the youth hostel stables on The

Ridgeway. Staying overnight with my favourite rider friends and the helpers was so much fun. Being able to open the bedroom door in the morning to see our horses in the stables opposite was amazing. Then hacking out on The Ridgeway all day, it was all my dreams come true.

Now I think we can all agree, being disabled is pretty rubbish right? But there is a perk, there is a rather exclusive club called The RDA. They operate a strict door policy: if you ain't disabled, you ain't getting in (or something along those lines).

Becoming a member of the RDA, didn't just make me feel better about being disabled, it actually made me glad that I was. All the things I couldn't do, no longer mattered. Thanks to Abingdon RDA, look at all the things I could now do, look at what I was a part of, look at where I belonged. The adventures, the holidays, the things I got to see, do and experience, enriched my life so much, that there was no way I'd trade all of that for a working body thanks!

I stupidly went AWOL during my teenage years, and only returned to the stables 6 months ago. I can't remember the exact head count that it took to get me (and my colourful language) back in the saddle again. Let's just say there was a flock of wonderful women (you've seen them, always got a twinkle in their eye and a spring in their step) all totally invested in me and making it happen. And it did! But it was absolute agony, I was totally disheartened. I had to return the next week though, I could not let the flock down. And do you know what? Although I'd been missing from the stables for 30 years, my 4 year old face was in a photo on the toilet wall! I'm eternally grateful to everyone that has contributed to making Abingdon RDA the wonderful place it is. If you hear on the news of a woman on horseback racing down the A420, that will be me - 'borrowing' Lisa or Rosie or maybe even Harry.... I will bring them back for my next lesson, I promise.

THE JOY OF TEAMWORK

by Amanda Graham

A very windy night in the big arena, second week back after Christmas. I just watched a helper combination of Mother and daughter (around 14) having the time of their lives working with one of our most engaging riders.

They were singing, making up stories, bantering (I heard the daughter make a suggestion, and the Mother say "oooo get her!"). And of course doing some great riding.

If you ever wanted to see joy in a bundle, then this was it.

I went over and said, "Team M, how is Bobby (the horse) tonight? Is he going to run away with you?" The rider started to answer then said to the helpers "you say". "Bobby's not going anywhere" said one of the helpers.

This was a fair question from me, as when I asked a similar question the previous week "How do you feel about Bobby trotting?" the answer was a resounding no. (That's what the Christmas break does, takes a week or two to settle in again).

"So, off the lead then?" Downturned face from rider. "Awwww it'll be fine, they'll stay close."

And they did, and the rider rose to the challenge and some wonderful circles appeared!

I will remember for a long time the joy that that 3 person team and Bobby brought tonight. Our final move was a very long trot around the whole arena. When I said, OK cool down the lesson is over, downturned face from rider again. "I don't want to stop".

Doesn't get much better than that.

MY EXPERIENCE OF RIDING A HORSE

by Alina Maria Dina (aged 11)

When I first started riding I was very excited about riding a horse. The horse that I was riding was a good horse, his name was Jasper, but another horse caught my attention, her name was Candy. I wanted to ride her because she was a girl. I started to think she was a good girl and we both became best friends and I loved her so much. I loved going on hacks with her because we got to see other views of the fields and other horses. One day there was a virus known as Covid and I could not see Candy, but one day I could see her and I was so happy

to see her again I fed her a carrot on a plate and an apple. Then I groomed her. After Covid there was competition and we had to help getting our horses ready for the competition, we got to clean their feet and horseshoes, it was so fun then we groomed them. It's time for the competition!
Guess what? I won first place!

We had so much fun, a lot of years passed, and sadly Candy was put down because of old age. I was so angry but at night I started to cry because I would not see her again.

As the years went by I started to ride a new horse called Plum and she's my best friend like Candy.

HIGHLIGHTS OF ABINGDON GROUP TAKEN FROM THE MINUTES 1975 - 1995

1975

March

Group Committee formed to run Oxford and District Group under the Chairmanship of Wendy Payne. One class of adults from the Oxford Handicapped Centre started at Steventon at the South Oxfordshire Equitation Centre.

April

Bennett House and Tesdale Schools started on Boars Hill.

June

Physically Handicapped children's evening class started at Steventon, Elaine Madley.

September

Ann Barlow elected Chairman upon resignation of Wendy Payne.

1976

February

Annual costs for digging estimated at £426.

7th November. Name changed to Abingdon Group.

1978

April

Moved to Lovells Court Farm Riding School, Hinton Waldrist, except for Boars Hill classes.

2nd September. Class for physically handicapped children started.

1979

May

Started driving in the summer months.

1980

Bennett House and Tesdale schools moved to Lovells Court due to closure of Riding School, Boars Hill.

1981

Big fund raising target set for this 'International Year of the Disabled' £800 from Children in Need.
Decided to try and find our own yard to rent.
October. Moved to Wadley Manor. Fees up to £1 per hour. Jane Viner employed and 2 ponies bought.

1982

5 more ponies owned by Group.
Indoor school refurbished and extended by RAF Benson free of charge.
Change of ownership of Wadley.

1983

Further extension of indoor school (£789).

Part time employee taken on.

1985

Anna Hearnden qualifies for National Dressage Championships and wins.
Start to consider building our own premises.

1987

Continue search for land.
Georgia Allen joint winner of National Dressage Championships at Weston Park.
Offer of land from J.C. Lewis Partnership at Lower Lodge, Longworth.

1988

Autumn

Work commences on indoor school, stables etc and appeal is launched.

1989

May. Move to Lower Lodge Riding Centre.
Appeal target £52,747. Cost of project £66,700.
October. Opening of Centre by The Princess

Royal.

1990

Public Address system installed. Lorry given by Wantage Round Table.

1991

Sprinkler system installed. Viewing gallery/ mounting ramp completed.
Summer driving group started at Goosey Wick Farm.

1993

Extension for extra stalls completed (£6,681.70)
Started riding on the Ridgeway.

1994

Spring. Vaulting started.
113 Riders and Drivers.
92 Voluntary Helpers.
16 Instructors.
14 Riding Classes - 2 at White Horse Stables, Goosey, 2 Driving Classes at White Horse Stables, Goosey, 1 Vaulting class.
Expenditure 1994 - £1,947

Blacksmith - £799
Building - £6,832
No administration costs, all money directly into the Centre.
Annual running cost approximately £18, 000. All income fundraising or donations from the public.

In comparison the current (2024) statistics are as follows:

14 qualified coaches, 2 coaches in training, plus 1 paid coach
14 riding sessions for around 70 riders. 94 volunteers

Expenditure for 2024 was £106,467.00
(Plus) Farrier £5605.70 and Buildings £5302.14

There are now lots of administration costs and income comes from lessons and arena hire as well as fund raising and donations from the public.

NEVER WORK WITH CHILDREN OR ANIMALS…

by Angy Irvin

One of the many jobs a coach needs to do is to train helpers. This usually takes place in and around normal lessons but on occasion we will organise a separate event. It happened that just as we had an influx of new helpers, the horses needed a week off so we took the opportunity to arrange some helper training without the distraction of riders and a "normal" lesson.

The session was arranged and as part of the plan we were going to cover "leading a pony correctly". We reached that part of the evening and I explained this was what was going to happen next to the expectant group of helpers.

I confidently put the head collar and lead rope on Bobby who was waiting patiently in his stall. At this point Bobby, a 12.2HH Welsh bay pony thought he was going to be turned out to the field. As I released him from his stall to walk across to the school, he tried to walk in the direction of his field. I stopped him and tried to lead him towards the school. Bobby decided that that definitely was not where he was going and went in the opposite direction at speed! I was carted across the loafing area and eventually let go!

A fine example of how to lead a pony!!! Once Bobby had made his point he was happy to be caught and behaved well for the training session! It just goes to show you should never work with children or animals and doing both leads to you looking like an idiot on a regular basis!!

ANGY IRVIN

RDA STORY

by Anonymous

Have you met a baby that doesn't cry? Not because they can't cry; not because they are content? A baby so neglected that they no longer believe crying will cause an adult to soothe, to comfort?

Research indicates a child neglected in the first weeks of life then moved to safety for the next twelve years will have worse outcomes than a child well cared for in the first weeks but then left in an unsafe setting for the next twelve years. Babies who are not rocked, cuddled and soothed do not grow the brain synapses needed to feel safe in their own body. Years on, and this neglect has left its mark.

My (adopted) daughter is impulsive from the moment she wakes. Everyday. When she is feeling safest she can't leave my side; when she is feeling least safe she pushes me away. She is hypervigilant of her environment; yet unaware of her own body signals. She is unable to control how much pressure to apply to her limbs. Her brain believes she is unsafe, where what is safe or unsafe was defined in those first days when adults were not there to help. Still, often, she can't ignore a stranger; she needs to control the attention of everyone present to manage the risk they present. It dominates all her relationships. Feeling worthy of care is something only other people deserve. She tells me she is stupid multiple times each day.

She doesn't feel seen. Almost every adult she meets infers it is her choice to feel or react this way; too few people understand that damage to the instinctive, reptilian part of our brain that grows fastest in the first months of life can't be overcome by wanting to react as others do. She can't, rather than won't. For a while, she chose to pray to God every night asking him to help her stop hurting people.

But, put her on a horse, and magic happens. The difference is so remarkable that sometimes I feel uncomfortable that it's not obvious why she has been given a place at RDA. The fear doesn't evaporate; the adrenaline in her limbs still makes it hard not to kick repeatedly, not to talk incessantly making instructions unclear, not to pull the reins in too far. She presses on the brake and the accelerator simultaneously. But the genuine joy on her face when on a horse doesn't happen anywhere else. Her posture looks more relaxed than in any other setting. And a girl who doesn't value herself enough to express opinions – to have a favourite colour, or a favourite anything - has found a passion in horses. She is motivated to learn, to risk failure, not to simply follow the crowd.

RIDING

by Caitlin Cartledge (aged 9)

I love going to Abingdon RDA and riding horses.

I got my Grade 2 in horse care and riding at the beginning of August.

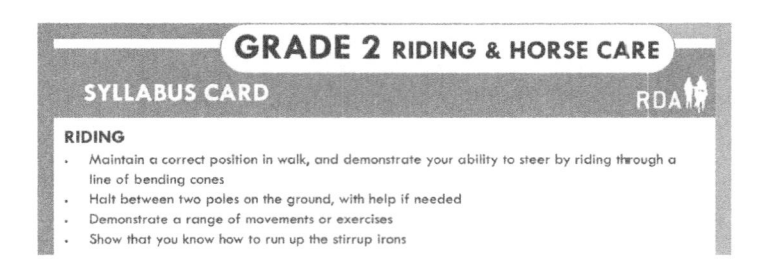

> **GRADE 2 RIDING & HORSE CARE**
> **SYLLABUS CARD** RDA
>
> **RIDING**
> - Maintain a correct position in walk, and demonstrate your ability to steer by riding through a line of bending cones
> - Halt between two poles on the ground, with help if needed
> - Demonstrate a range of movements or exercises
> - Show that you know how to run up the stirrup irons

I took part in the Funday when I rode Elbow and a Pony Morning in the summer holidays where I rode Plum. It was lots of fun. I got rosettes that I love showing to my family and keep in my room.

Since I starting at Abingdon RDA I have ridden Harry, Plum, Lisa, Rosie, Marshall and Elbow. My favourite horses to ride are Lisa, Rosie and Plum – I love their colours.

RDA AND WHAT IT MEANS TO US

By Nikki Busby (drawing by Alex Busby, aged 9)

When lockdockdown hit the UK everyone massively struggled, but for us with a SEND child we became prisoners in our own home. We couldn't get out for fresh air walks like the other families and even when rules were lifted, we still felt like prisoners. My autistic and non-verbal son, Jake, was left with severe anxiety issues that made him too afraid to leave the house, too afraid to see his grandparents, too afraid to be hugged by anyone and even too afraid to have anyone visit our home.

Every trip outside our house, no matter how small, became a battle and it became easier to just give in and stay at home rather than take Jake out and have to deal with his meltdowns. Our family was at breaking point.

School never saw the meltdowns we had to endure with Jake because school remained a daily routine for him. It soon became very clear that further routine was what was so desperately needed for Jake and our family.

I cried when we were offered weekly lessons at Abingdon. Since Jake has been visiting RDA our little boy is now thriving. Jake's speech has started to develop enormously and he is now starting to string sentences together which is just amazing and something we did not think would ever be possible for him to do. He now leaves the house and thoroughly looks forward to visiting RDA every week. His core muscles have improved so much and he now interacts more at home with family and friends. RDA is always at the forefront of Jake's thinking.

RDA has given us so many happy days and has saved our little boy from the fear of the outside world. He is now part of a group that accepts him for being himself which is priceless. Our little boy is finally happy and thriving thanks to Abingdon RDA.

CANTER ON MR B

by Sue Murrin

One summer evening the ride were out at the top of the front field practising for the handy pony competition which would be part of Funday in a few weeks' time.

All the riders were doing their thing when dear Mr B who had been doing this for weeks decided he had had enough.

At the end of the trotting lane he caught his young rider by surprise and headed off back to the yard at a very laid back canter.

His young rider could do nothing but sit and enjoy the ride - her first canter - something she will never forget.

LOVELY LISA

by Lily Mae Pearce (aged 10)

One Saturday I arrived at RDA and headed straight for the tack room. Bea (trainee coach) was in there and she said to me, "You're riding a new pony, Lisa today!"

I was so excited I practically ran to the Barlow Arena and sat on the mini grand stadium.

As soon as the beautiful, piebald (black and white), Lisa entered the arena I jumped down from where I was sitting and walked towards her took her reins and led her to the mounting block. I got on and Bea sorted my girth and stirrups then she offered to lead me around the arena and I accepted as I was a little bit nervous. As we walked around the arena Bea told me everything I needed to know about Lisa.

PURPOSE IN LIFE

by Tim Stimpson

As a supporter of RDA and on one of my early visits to the Abingdon riding stables, I spotted an elderly gentleman who was helping around the yard in his wet weather gear.

As my visit unfolded and due to the horrible British weather, we were moved into one of the indoor arenas. Soon after, the gentleman I had seen came inside to shelter from the worsening storm, conversation ensued, and I soon learned that the gentleman was in remission from cancer after a lengthy spell of chemotherapy.

When I asked what made him want to come out in the horrendous weather to volunteer, he responded with a few words that will stay with me. He said,

"The camaraderie and the work that I do is valued by the users and by seeing the smiles on the riders faces, it gives me purpose in life to keep going."

Well done that man!

THE FUNDAY AND I CAME FOURTH!

By Sarah Heyburn (age 8)

My name is Sarah and I go to Abingdon Rda, a few monts ago it was the fundays and I came forth. My favter pony is bryn he is so gentle and kind and I also love trroting. yesterday we did dressarge I got a sticker and so did Bryn. we put it on his nose band it was so funny we got a photo. I have had so much fun here thank you bryn.

My name is Sarah and I go to Abingdon RDA. A few months ago it was the funday and I came fourth. My favourite pony is Bryn, he is so gentle and kind and I also love trotting.

Yesterday we did dressage I got a sticker and so did Bryn! We put it on his noseband, it was so funny we got a photo. I have had so much fun here. Thank you Bryn.

THE ADVENTURES OF HARRY AND MARSHALL

by Jo Sproston

It was a late summer's day at Abingdon Group RDA. Riders had been for their lessons and, work completed, all the horses and ponies had been turned out in their fields.

We do not know whether the leader was Harry or Marshall but one of these ponies noticed that the field was not quite properly secured and with a little bit of helpful persuasion they could open the gateway and leave their designated grazing area!

Luckily for the human helpers these ponies were not interested in a grand adventure to distant shores, their goal was much closer, some very tasty bushes that they usually could not get to; bushes that had probably never before been snacked on by a pony!

As their neared their goal Marshall noted "Oh no, this wooden box is in the way."

Harry replied "Pffft, no problem, we can squeeze through there!"

So the ponies breathed in and agilely worked their way around the box to find themselves at the base of a short, but quite steep, slope with the tasty looking bushes tempting them from the top.

As they stood at the base of the slope Marshall declared "Oh! This slope looks much steeper than I thought."

"That?" responded Harry, "Pffft, that's no problem. Here follow me, I used to know a donkey and he taught me all he knew. I'm as nimble as a mountain goat!"

So Harry sets off up the slope with Marshall close behind. Making surprisingly quick work of the slope they are soon rewarded with their tasty treats. It was a very tight squeeze for both of the ponies to fit on the grassy ledge at the top of the bank; and they had to take it in turns browsing in the bushes.

The ponies had only a few minutes to enjoy their flavoursome prize before a human helper spotted the escapees.

"Oh no!" declared Harry, "One of the hoomans is coming this way, squish in here, if we're still and really close to the bushes they might not see us."

"Too late" replied Marshall "Look she's gone to get the others, and they're heading this way."

The helpers had indeed spotted the mischievous ponies and armed with headcollars and lead ropes they had made their way to the bottom of the slope where they were considering how on earth they were going to safely encourage the ponies back down the slope. It was decided that the close quarters meant just one helper should make their way to the ponies to assess from the top and see if they could pick a careful pathway back down the slope.

Harry resumed eating as no-one was making him stop just yet. "Well it looks like they really are going to ruin our fun!" he said to Marshall, "I'm just going to push down here a bit and see if I can gobble some extra treats before they make it up here!"

As the ponies had before her, the helper tried to make her way up the slope. Unfortunately, it was more slippery than it looked and took some careful negotiation.

Marshall watched the humans carefully, "At least it's taking them a while, this helper doesn't seem as nimble as we are" he said to Harry.

Harry replied "I keep telling everyone that 4 legs are so much better than 2!"

Finally, safely at the top, the helper could only reach Marshall but, being a very good boy, he happily accepted his headcollar, waited patiently for the helper to make progress in returning down the slope and then carefully followed, taking care not to step on her! Once Marshall was safely back on flat ground it was time for the helper to, hopefully, make a second successful ascent. Harry continued to snack as much as he could keeping a careful eye on the approaching helper.

"I'm glad she's so slow" thought Harry, "this bush is decidedly tasty." As the helper made it to the top for a second time, Harry grabbed one last delicious mouthful before his headcollar was put on and he and the helper cautiously turned to face back down the slope. At this point the helper suddenly disappeared!

Harry looked down, and down some more. There was the helper sitting on the floor a little way down the slope, having slipped on the uneven ground and plopped onto the floor.

"Well" thought Harry, "she definitely doesn't have her mountaineering badge! At least if I didn't get more snacks I got a good laugh. Oh and look, her helper friend is trying to get a photo, how helpful of her!"

Happily Harry stood nicely and waited for the helper to get safely down the slope and into a place where he could easily pass her. Then Harry, demonstrating his best mountain goat impression, expertly and nimbly scampered down the bank and obediently stopped next to the helper:

"I'd better wait just here in case she needs a hand, I don't think she's anywhere near as fleet-footed as me" thought Harry.

The helper gave Harry a pat, telling him he was both an "absolute menace" and a "really good boy". Both ponies were returned to their grazing paddock. The field closure was checked, not once, not twice but 3 times and the gates firmly locked. So Harry and Marshall's short but sweet adventure was over, for now…..

BINGO IN THE BARLOW ARENA

By Nikki Busby

As a fundraising volunteer the first event I organised was a bingo night but with a unique unplanned twist. I wanted to hold an event in the Barlow Arena at Abingdon RDA to help raise awareness of the premises and to let everyone see the beautiful grounds. A lot of planning and work went into organising this event. A lorry was hired collecting 90 chairs and tables from Oxford. Prizes were donated and collected far and wide from supporting businesses. Hot pasties and sausage rolls were available to purchase on the night, a car park attendant was arranged to help us comply with health and safety as identified in the risk assessment and the bingo was advertised extensively. In the run up to the event we started to release some of the top prizes to help draw people into the event with daily updates being posted.

On the day, the team of volunteers spent around 3 hours transforming the Barlow Arena into a bingo hall, we were exhausted. About an hour before the doors were due to open and just as we were thinking we could head home to get changed and have a well-deserved cup of tea, the power went down. NIGHTMARE! It soon transpired that the power would be out for some time. With phones in hand, volunteers started to ring round friends and family to try and get hold of some generators, but with the time now at about 16.00 on a Saturday afternoon, the suggestion of cancelling did cross our minds. I was now having a complete panic attack underneath the calm exterior thinking how do we continue? To cancel was unthinkable - it would have been pretty much impossible to reach everyone to let them know that the bingo could not go ahead.

In the true spirit of fundraising, a message was put out in the hope to reach everyone to tell them to bring torches, battery lights, phones - anything they could get hold of to give some light and to pass the message on. We were totally amazed at the number of people who offered to help and even more astonished about how many people then turned up, 193 to be precise. We ran out of chairs and tables, but again problem solved, hay bales were brought out for people to sit on and use as tables. Everyone thoroughly enjoyed themselves and said how much fun it had been to play bingo by torchlight. It was a very successful night enjoyed by all. We can laugh about it now and look back on the memories created. Bingo by torchlight raised a staggering £1826.16. Along with a £1000 cheque donation from someone who saw our bingo advert, could not attend the event, but still wanted to support. This gave us a grand total of £2826.16.

Did this put me off helping to fundraise? No, it has made me believe that with a team of fabulous volunteers anything is possible. We have even been asked to hold another fundraising bingo by torchlight!

RIDGEWAY MEMORIES

by Lyndsey Trickett

I have many happy memories of my 14 years involvement with Abingdon RDA.

I particularly enjoyed the rides we used to go on up on The Ridgeway. Up until a few years ago every August, our ponies were taken up to a farm on the edge of The Ridgeway for a week's holiday and we would go and ride them up there. I think the ponies enjoyed their break and our rides as much as we did. My usual Ridgeway buddy was our legendary all-rounder Speckles. An added bonus of these rides was that I usually rode on the same day as my good friend Sue Wakem who rode the equally legendary Rooster. On our day, we rode out for most of the day and had a picnic mid-way which gave the ponies a well-earned rest. We saw a lot of wildlife (and sheep) on our rides including butterflies and hares. We once noticed a red kite was sitting on a fence watching us go by. I will always treasure our time on The Ridgeway.

BRYN – ANGEL OR DEVIL?

by Angy Irvin

Bryn is the smallest pony on the yard but one of the biggest characters. He is a favourite of one of my smallest riders – what they both lack in stature they make up for in character and cheek!

One week Bryn was giving his rider a lovely confidence building ride, obeying her slightly wobbly commands and generally being a perfect RDA pony. His trot was slow and gentle and smooth as he could get it (leader was walking!), he stopped when asked, he braved going near the bucket so she could put a toy in (without checking for food!). Perfect.

"Is Bryn being good?" I asked the rider, "Yes she replied, he's a good boy." "Not always," I said and told her about the time a few weeks previously:

At turnout time, after the lesson, a group of helpers took the ponies to the new fields to be turned out. (For the uninitiated, the new fields are a line of adjacent paddocks separated by electric fencing). Bryn and his mates were in a field adjacent to three mares, two of whom were relatively new to RDA. Once released Bryn galloped at full steam across the field to the fence (followed by his mates), calmly ducked underneath the top string and pushed his way through the bottom one to join the mares! The rest of the geldings fortunately stayed in the correct field. The mares, not taking too kindly to Bryn's advances (he's not exactly hunky, bless him!) started chasing him off. At once helpers mobilised to catch Bryn (he wasn't having any of that – thank you!) and mend the fence. Eventually, with the help of rustling sweet papers in a helpers' pocket, Bryn was caught and escorted back to the correct field none the worse for his adventure.

As I told the rider this story, I should have noticed the glint in Bryn's eye!

The lesson went well and once the riders had gone, it was once more turnout time. Bryn was given a hug as a thank you from his rider. This week, Bryn's allotted field was "Pig-mid", (which as the name suggests is the middle of a series of three paddocks named "the pig fields" – the reason for which is lost in the midst of time) and the furthest paddocks from the yard. Bryn was to be turned out with the 3 other smallest geldings Wizard, Jasper and Marshall, with JimBob (a big, unsociable cob) to occupy the field next to them. Fortunately we had enough help to turn out all five in one trip so once they were rugged up we set off down to the field. JimBob and his leader stayed in the first field whilst the others were led through to the next field. Once there they were released. All four galloped off joyously (which I love to watch), except that Bryn kept going through the fence into the next field!

This time he didn't break the fence as he went through the gateway but it was closed – with the wires across! OK. Time to consider the options: leave him there? No – too much spring grass for one small pony! Open the gate to let all four ponies have both fields? No – still too much grass for four small ponies! Move the other three into the field Bryn preferred? No - JimBob would be completely on his own! Catch Bryn and move him back? The only option but definitely not the easiest! A helper was dispatched to get some food... Meanwhile I tried to catch him. He would let me approach and even sniffed my hand but once he knew it was empty of food he trotted off out of reach. Again, and again and again. Then he trotted towards the gateway (the wires were up to make sure the other three ponies remained where they were supposed to be). A quick thinking helper started to undo the gate for him, but before she could do so he pushed his way through the fence back into his field. Fortunately the fence remained intact. A quick phone call to the helper fetching food "we don't need the food but put the electric fence on quick!", ensured that he remained where he was for the rest of the night (I hoped!).

RDA AND ME

by Chloe Humphreys

When I first joined the RDA Abingdon Group, I thought it would just be a couple of hours a week helping others, getting to spend some time around horses, and hopefully making a few friends. Little did I know what a big part of my life it would become! Suddenly, going to the yard was something I looked forward to every week, and I found myself wanting to get more involved.

Fast forward two years, and now I'm helping manage Saturday lessons, training as a coach, part of the fundraising team, designing our newsletter, and running our social media pages. Knowing that I'm getting to help others fills me with pride and fulfilment. There's just something magical about seeing the riders' faces light up and knowing I've been a part of that joy. RDA has given me confidence, new skills, an amazing group of friends, and a true sense of purpose. It's no longer just a place I volunteer, it's a big part of my life that I couldn't imagine being without!

ABINGDON RIDING FOR THE DISABLED

by Tim Stimpson MBE

Disabled or disadvantaged, should not get in the way.
A place was created known as Abingdon RDA.

A place where volunteering is at the heart of its work.

Seeing our users develop comes naturally, it's a perk.

Our users are delighted which brings a smile and a tear,

In a world where fund raising gets harder each year.

Our ever-increasing overheads just seem to rocket.

We know it's a big ask to donate cash from your pocket.

Our grant funding gets capped at about a third.

Users pay for our service, without a cross word.

Annual fundraising is how Abingdon RDA needs to survive.

Please could you donate to help us thrive and provide?

However small, please can you make us a donation.

Helping us maintain this unique horse rider relation.

MY DRAWING

By Hazel Frith (age 5)

Can you see Bryn's lovely tail?

CHEEKY JASPER

by Deborah Read

I recall a lesson we had with five little riders. The school was laid out with a gymkhana course and one of the games involved picking up a rubber duck and placing in a bucket of water.

Jasper (a cheeky, chestnut pony) decided to take an interest in the bobbing rubber ducks and managed to scoop one up in his mouth. The duck was rescued with some resistance from Jasper and the children all found this so funny as did the volunteers.

I am quietly confident that Jasper would not have eaten it!

The fun and games continued without the ducks, however Jasper decided this time he would try for a rubber ring hanging off the pole hooks. He found this slightly harder and in the end decided it was too much for him.

The following week the children were all keen to ride the gymkhana game again especially if Jasper was involved.

MY STORY

by Lesley Chaundy

I have been a Thursday night volunteer at Abingdon RDA since March 2017 and the time has flown by.

What started out as a horsey fix for me has turned out to be so much more - I have met some amazing people - coaches, volunteers, riders and parents and in doing so have learnt a lot and made good friends.

And then, the horses and ponies - what stars they are - all shapes, colours and sizes but all there to do a job and they do it well.

In the time I have been going I have seen how things have evolved and can see so many improvements. Iris came in like a whirlwind and things were labelled and tidied up making it so much easier to find what's needed and what belongs to each pony. Training of volunteers enhances rider and pony welfare and in addition a generous donation of new bridles for all the ponies meant that the use of headcollars under the old bridles was no longer necessary. The new arena - what an achievement that is and a testament to Ann Barlow.

It seems that Abingdon RDA is one whole with many working parts and it is a pleasure to be a part of it, however small.

SOME LESSONS ARE MORE EVENTFUL THAN OTHERS!

By Amanda Graham

It was the first lesson in a new academic year and we had a full house of five riders in the first lesson, including two new ones and four riders in the second lesson.

The night before a helper dropped out and, because we were near to the safe minimum number of helpers, I called around and found two helpers from other lessons who were happy to come and help us. In addition, one of the helpers from the new rider's previous lesson came to help with a smooth transition.

We planned the first lesson to be a "games" lesson and the second lesson to be a simple drill ride. Knowing that some of these riders had just had their first or second day at school in the new academic year, we were easing in gently - from experience we knew that they'd be tired and had been challenged during the day.

So what could possibly go wrong!

At 3:30, the yellow warning for rain turned into thunderstorms. And the rain came down in a torrent.

The first lesson was definitely off as far as riding was concerned and WhatsApp messages started flying. I tried to contact the helpers to stand some of them down but it was all too late they were on their way.

We got messages from some of the riders - "there is so much water on the road in front of us we don't think we can get out of the drive" and "with the summer disruption we forgot that we were back on tonight". So the wonderful extra helpers arrived but sadly were redundant but, as ever with RDA helpers, they were good about it and just got on with sorting horses and the yard.

We ended up switching horses around for the second lesson, so that 1) some horses could get turned out and 2) we didn't use Harry because he seriously does not like the sound of rain on the arena roof and he was pretty jumpy.

The first lesson went ahead as an unmounted lesson. The new riders had a wonderful game on the gallery with the rest of the class that arrived. As we all know, RDA is not just about riding and that initial familiarisation and bonding was a real bonus for the new riders, and they had great fun too!

Having consulted a pilot who is excellent at reading the weather and looking at my lightning strike app I decided that the second lesson could go ahead. A simple drill ride. That was until Rosie and Maple decided otherwise! Having had two weeks off for the summer they were very, very forward and it took nearly half the lesson to get them calm enough to attempt this drill ride, the helpers, as ever, were just brilliant.

When all was calmer, Angy and I demonstrated the first shape of the drill ride on foot. All good. Then having achieved this we increased the complexity to a crossover of the horses at X. We needed to demonstrate this again mainly because one of the riders said she didn't quite understand the shape. So as we were now running short of time, Angy and I ran the route. Little did I know that Angy decided she wanted to make me run fast! I was demonstrating being the first horse to X and she was crossing behind me and I could see her running fast at me so I had to run faster. When we got back to the horses, I could see that, the riders and helpers were all laughing hysterically at our antics.

Finishing off the evening turning out the horses, we heard a bang from one of the stables. Elbow was being kept inside a stable because she had laminitis. We had turned out the other mares into a field close by but not next to her stable, and she decided not close enough! She jumped over the stable door to get into a paddock closer to them and was running around the paddock rearing and bucking (which is not great for a horse with laminitis). Angy immediately got a feed bucket with a small amount of feed in it and rattled it around to bring her in and calm her down. We contacted Iris and asked advice and she said well you can leave Elbow out in the very small paddock if she's feeling that well! and bring the other mares towards her so they are only separated by the fence. The perfect end to an RDA evening!

If there are any RDA coaches reading this, you will recognise this as a hectic evening full of adaptability and flexibility but in fairness, not that unusual. Life as an RDA coach is wonderful, challenging, a bit stressful (as one of my helpers had said earlier in the evening "you're looking a bit flustered"!) and probably one of the best jobs in the world.

ME AND RANGER

by Megan Marriott

My story is about me and Ranger back in May 2018 - July 3rd 2019.

It all started when I got assigned Ranger for the RDA Regional Show in 2018. I was so happy as Ranger was my favourite horse. We practised for weeks to prepare so we would be ready for the show. I remember when I went to the show and I did my test I was so happy. I felt like it went really well. Then the time came at prize giving they announced "and in first place for grade 7 Walk and Trot is Megan Marriott from Abingdon RDA." I was so very happy. I couldn't believe it! That was the first time I ever won at the Regionals. Winning the Regional competition meant that I was eligible for the RDA National Championship competition.

Then the time came to practise for the National

Championships. This was my first time ever going to the Championships but I couldn't have been happier as it was with my favourite horse Ranger, a horse in a million. I remember all the practise we did. I also remember I had my first canter on Ranger when practising for RDA National Championships. It felt so amazing! I couldn't imagine having my first canter in over 2 years on any other horse. I loved him so much and I couldn't wait to show the judges at Nationals what we had improved on since the Regionals when we came 1st out of 8 riders. I remember going into the arena and thinking let's give it all we have got. When we did the test, it felt so good, like we had really shown how we had improved. We did our best and we came 10th out of 24. I couldn't have been happier. I am so happy that my 2 best achievements were with Ranger.

Then 5 months later the time came to stop riding as I needed to go into hospital for spinal fusion treatment to correct my scoliosis on December 13th 2018. I remember how devastated I was knowing it could be 18 months before I would be able to ride Ranger again. I remember the first time I saw Ranger after my back surgery. He ignored me and wouldn't come up and say hi in the field. But time passed and although it took three months to get there, I was back on the yard spending time with Ranger and the other horses, enjoying grooming them all. Two and a half months later,

I was back riding the horses, after only five and a half months off.

But Ranger couldn't be ridden as he had only just had surgery for a twisted gut due to having colic. Sadly only four weeks after that Ranger ended up passing away from complications from the previous surgery. This was on the 3rd of July 2019 and it was when my life changed forever. I didn't know if I was ever going to bond with another horse again. I love horses, but it took me five and a half years to start to bond with another horse in the same way. This horse is called Lisa. She has got me through and showed me that it was ok to love another horse.

I guess the moral of the story is to never give up on your dreams and never stop thinking about what you learnt with your horse of a lifetime. I will always love you and miss you Ranger. You will never be forgotten.

PONY TALES 2 MORE MEMORIES OF ABINGDON RDA

A LETTER TO BRYN

by Isabella Chandler (aged 7)

A Letter to Bryn

Dear Bryn

I love riding you because you trot very fast and it makes me smile.
You help me ride very well because you listen to me.
I cuddle you because your coat is so soft.
The colour of your coat is like my dogs.
You are very kind and I care for you a lot.
You have given me lots of friends.

I love your kisses after a lesson because they make me laugh.

love from

Bella

Dear Bryn

I love riding you because you trot very fast and it makes me smile. You help me ride very well because you listen to me. I love to cuddle you because your coat is so soft. The colour of your coat is like my dog's. You are very kind and I care for you a lot. You have given me lots of friends. I love your kisses after a lesson because they make me laugh.

Love from

Bella xxxxxxxxxxxxxxxxxxxxxxxxxxxxxxxxxxx

RIDING

by Michael Cartledge
(aged 9)

I like going to Abingdon RDA because I like riding and I like my horse Rosie.

I love Rosie's colour and how tall I am when I ride Rosie.

I enjoy being able to brush Rosie and take off her tack at the end of my lesson.

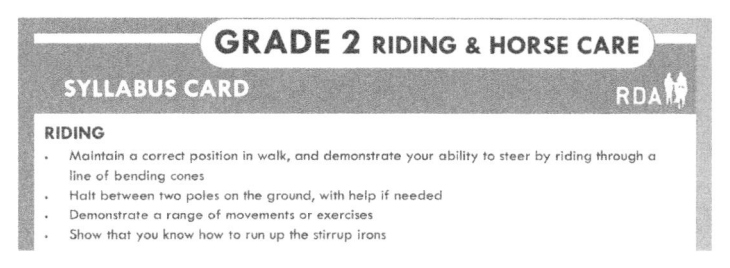

> **GRADE 2 RIDING & HORSE CARE**
> **SYLLABUS CARD** RDA
>
> **RIDING**
> - Maintain a correct position in walk, and demonstrate your ability to steer by riding through a line of bending cones
> - Halt between two poles on the ground, with help if needed
> - Demonstrate a range of movements or exercises
> - Show that you know how to run up the stirrup irons

At Abingdon RDA I got my Grade 2 certificates for

riding and horse care and I took part in the Funday and Pony Day which I really enjoyed. I got rosettes for taking part which I put in my room so I can see them and show my family and friends.

BRAVE ROSIE

by Angy Irvin

Rosie is a large (ish) chestnut mare and was not originally suitable for use in our lessons due to her stature. However, children grow and circumstances change so we decided to try her out for one of our teenage riders. Never having used her in a lesson or seen her being ridden (except briefly on the Funday) I had some qualms about using her. (She doesn't look like your standard RDA horse, not being a cob.)

On this particular evening she was happily grazing in the field when we arrived with her two companions. Armed with a headcollar, I set out to catch her. Unfortunately Rosie was not in the mood to be caught and would gently wander off out of reach every time I got close to her and hide behind Prin and Maple. Time before lessons is precious, so spending 10-15 minutes catching her in the gathering dusk was not on my to do list! Just as I was about to admit defeat and go and find some bribery (ie. food) she decided that she was willing to do some work that evening and allowed me to catch hold of her! Not the best start…

I planned to spend 10-15 minutes riding her before the lesson to "get the feel of her" and settle her down before the rider arrived, so we duly groomed and tacked her up and I got onboard. My first thoughts were "She's tall" – she's over 16hh and I hadn't ridden for a while. It was dark by this time and the indoor school was full of shadows (even with the lights on). She was lovely to ride very responsive although she was quite "spooky" finding imaginary scary things in the shadows by the tack room and on the gallery. Hmmm, I hope the rider can handle that I thought…fingers crossed!

The lesson began and the rider mounted (we gave her our most competent leader). All went well. Rosie performed perfectly throughout the lesson, doing everything her rider asked of her calmly and safely. The rider loved her and a promising new partnership was formed.

After the lesson, the leader mentioned to me how tense Rosie was at times during the lesson but she (Rosie) was absolutely determined that she wouldn't spook and upset the rider. She carried her safely despite being scared herself! What a brave girl – she wouldn't upset one of our riders but knew she was ok to spook with me!

WASHING BRYN

By Tilly O'Shea (age 5)

I love Bryn. I love washing the horse's with a sponge and water.

Caroline is holding Bryn.

Daisy is my favourite too.

Tilly's words with Mummy writing.

RIDER AND PARENT'S VIEWS

by Jenny and Rob Pace

Jenny's Words On RDA:

I like going to the RDA because I have made new friends and I have learned to ride a pony. Bobby is my favourite pony but I'm not sure why I like him. The volunteers are quite nice, and one of them has the same birthday as me. Learning to ride a pony has made me more brave.

Parents Words On RDA:

As a parent of a child with hypotonia amongst other issues we were always looking out for activities to try to improve core strength, stability & balance. Pony riding was not something we'd ever thought of but we were intrigued after seeing the work of group highlighted on Countryfile! We joined a lovely small group and came along every week to sit in the school and watch the other children riding. Over time she started to grow in confidence and we began to touch and stroke the ponies and months after first going to watch she finally allowed herself to be lifted to sit on a pony! From then it's had a huge impact on confidence and core stability. We now ride confidently and love trotting around the arena with our pony. The volunteers are incredible and are so patient, really helping the children to make the most of their sessions. We've loved our time with the RDA - the confidence gained has been fabulous. Thanks RDA!

MY RDA STORY

by Karen Stubbs

I first came across the RDA in April 2000. I have always loved horses and been fortunate enough to own my own. Within a couple of years, I became a coach and over the years I have worked with both children and adults. It gives me great pleasure to see people grow in confidence, learn new skills, have fun and just be themselves. The work of the RDA is something that I passionately believe in, the connection between horses and people is very special. As well as coaching, I enjoy training and helping other coaches, which is my role as a County Coach and next year I will be taking on the role of Regional Coach.

It is so rewarding to be able to help people to feel better about themselves or improve their skills through riding and help them to achieve goals that they didn't think they could attain.

Some quotes from some of my riders and their families.
"Thank you for giving me the belief in myself to ride again"
"The highlight of my week,"
"I never thought that she could achieve anything like this"
"It makes me the same as everyone else"

Every rider is different and you learn as much from them as they do from you.
Abingdon RDA will celebrate its 50th Anniversary in 2025 and as the Group Chairman, I hope that we will continue to enrich lives through horses for many years to come.

MINTY SMELL

by Lorrie Dinger

A few weeks ago we were tacking up for the Tuesday morning pre-school Group.

As we led the ponies out, Christine arrived to help. Suddenly Bryn, Marshall and Harry pulled over towards Christine and started nudging her and wanting to look in her pockets.

I asked her if she had polo mints in her pockets and she said "No my pockets are empty!!"

The ponies continued to want to follow her in the arena until she suddenly worked out why!

Earlier in the day she had applied some peppermint back rub to her sore back and of course the ponies could smell the peppermint!!!

WALKING ON MY OWN

by Isaac Grange (Age 8)

The first pony I rode was Bryn and I started off wearing a special belt that the sidewalkers would hold on to so I wouldn't fall off.

Since then I've got a lot better at horseriding and my body is much stronger. Just a few months ago and it is one of my favourite times, I rode Harry all by myself. It was the first time I had ever ridden without side walkers. I was thinking "Oh my days I'm walking on my own, what if I fall!" but I didn't, I loved it and I felt really proud of myself. I remember standing up in front of my whole school in assembly that week to show the video my mum took of it because it was such an achievement for me.

I want to say a massive thank you to RDA, to my coaches, the volunteers who have helped me and of course the ponies!

THANK YOU RDA ABINGDON!

By Katherine Brimblecombe

My son has been riding at Abingdon RDA since he was 2 years old. We were referred by his physio after she noticed how well he responded to our pet cat Toby. Without Toby as a distraction, he was completely resistant to being touched at all for his exercises after his hip surgery. My son simply loves being around the horses and volunteers, he freely gives hugs and high-fives and will allow himself to be supported on the ponies. The highlight of his week is playing "grandmother's footsteps", trying his best to stay "statue still" until (our wonderful instructor) Jane turns around, his squeaks, smiles and flaps of joy are so infectious and it's so uplifting for me to watch. All the volunteers are brilliant and it's such a lift for us parents having people notice our children's "inchstone" improvements and celebrate them like family! Such a contrast to most of our appointments where we are forced to list short-comings that overlook all the amazing things that make up our disabled children. So, with my whole heart I say thank you to the instructors, volunteers, yard staff and of course ponies who encourage my beautiful boy to be his best self!

REMEMBERING LILY

by Angy Irvin

It was in the very early days of my teaching at RDA that I first met Lily.

Lily first came to RDA as a deaf little girl, who started her first riding in my Thursday evening classes.

Lily was small and dainty with a heart-shaped face who looked like a little angel. However she was very determined and knew her own mind. Qualities she would need throughout her too short life, especially when she was later diagnosed with mitochondrial disease, but qualities that made her somewhat daunting to teach for a new coach! I remember we had many discussions on how the reins should be held versus how Lily wanted to hold them and how a rider's leg should be positioned versus how Lily wanted to have her legs! Perhaps we both learnt to compromise! In any event, Lily made good progress and loved the horses and ponies.

Lily was only a year or so older than my children who she met at a funday. It was possibly her first funday and I was there helping out in a fairly limited way as I had both my children (under 5) with me. (I remember we mainly collected score sheets and distributed tea and biscuits to other volunteers!) When the riding was finished Lily and my children had a great time climbing up the mounting block and jumping off! Lily was wearing a gorgeous Spanish flamenco costume which she wore in the fancy dress competition. Although she was slightly older, she was smaller than both of my two, but determined that if they could climb on the block so could she.

Throughout the years she continued attending RDA and progressed well with her riding. She loved Charlie B and Speckles. She met a volunteer called Ian. They both had a wonderful time together, he was her "funny man" and they had a lot of fun in the lessons. Ian gave her the confidence and support she needed at a time when she could sense that she was becoming weaker instead of stronger as she grew.

Lily endured several spells in hospital and periods when she was too unwell to leave the house. She missed the ponies dreadfully. Fortunately for Lily, she lived close to the stables in Southmoor and on one occasion Speckles and a few human friends went to visit her! She absolutely loved having a pony come and see her, especially the characterful Speckles!

Eventually Lily grew too weak to ride and had to use a wheel chair. Her spirit and love of horses remained with her though. She especially loved Marshall and when she was well enough she came to visit him. He would stand for ages with his head in her lap whilst she petted him.

Sadly, we lost both Lily and her "funny man" Ian, within a few months of each other last summer. Hopefully somewhere they are reunited and having fun. RIP Lily and Ian.

MAPLE AND MARSHALL'S ADVENTURE

by Helene James-Menard

My name is Marshall and I am one of the amazing herd of ponies who live at Abingdon RDA. (I'm the small, handsome, black one with the white blaze.)

It was a normal Thursday. I was brought in from the field, had breakfast, carried a giggling child round during a lesson, but then Maple and I suspected something was brewing when one of our favourite humans, H, spent most of the rest of the day brushing and washing us. The next morning we followed her into a strange horsebox and prepared ourselves for our mystery adventure.

Though quite large, the horsebox had been filled with all sorts of paraphernalia. We could smell super clean tack, hay, bedding… and we could see some lesson equipment poking out above the partition. What was going on?

The journey was smooth but quite long. Especially towards the end when the lorry went slowly up and down hills, forwards and backwards, with wafts of all sorts of human food, drink, and new clothing drifting through the windows. Were our humans lost in a giant park full of shops? Finally the lorry stopped and we were led out into an attractive little wood. The first thing I noticed was the largest horse I had ever seen. You couldn't miss him! He was a Suffolk Punch over 18 hands high with a gorgeous bright chestnut summer coat. Maple was immediately besotted!

Our humans led us out of the wood to an area with some of the shops we had smelt, then to our surprise, into a stable each. The stables had luscious grass on the floor and a top quality view of an arena where all sorts of interesting things were happening. What a brilliant place!

People started walking past our stables and saying hello. When I felt like it, I let some of these friendly and curious strangers stroke and scratch me, I do like a fuss, but only when one of our humans was there to supervise and answer lots of questions about Maple and me. Turns out we were going to be stars in the arena! We were groomed to a brilliant shine, tacked up, then some of our best riders arrived and mounted next to the lorry away from the crowds. Indeed there were more people than I'd ever seen before walking and gathering around the arena. I felt quite nervous at first, but then I felt really proud demonstrating some of the lesson activities we do to help so many riders, whilst one of the coaches was commentating and explaining the history and role of the RDA to everyone. It was so exciting!

We had a little rest then completed another demonstration in the arena. Then the crowds began to disperse and things began to quieten. We noticed most of the humans had gone, ones we knew and the strangers, but thankfully H was still there, checking our water and even taking us out to the arena for a leg stretch and some yummy grass. She kept us fed and relaxed, and we knew she wouldn't be far if anything bad happened to us in this strange place. It was very pretty though. We could just about see a mansion across parkland behind which the sun set in a red flourish.

The next day we completed a couple more demonstrations. One was really exciting because a helicopter took off from just outside the arena. Our humans thought it would be a good idea to demonstrate dismounting and mounting our riders because we had never seen one of these noisy metal flying things so close! Other fascinating new experiences included watching lots of hunt hounds, pony club activities, Suffolk Punch carriages, polo demos, terriers, birds of prey, all in the arena in front of us.

After the crowds dispersed towards the end of the second day we were glad to get back on the lorry. All the excitement was quite tiring and we knew our friends back home would wish to hear all about our adventure. We were so pleased to have represented the RDA to many people at the Blenheim Palace Game Fair, showing them some of

ANGY IRVIN

the amazing work we do every day.

SHUSH!

By Jo Sproston

My worklife requires me to spend a lot of time communicating with other people. Much talking and creating data packets and trying to convey lots of information to a varied audience i.e. a lot of talking and listening. And, as anyone with these types of tasks as part of a role will tell you, there's oft quoted statistics about "more than 50% of communication is body language" and "less than 10% of communication is about what you actually say" along with other considerations like practising active listening and staying present and "on task". Well, if ever these terms and considerations seem too abstract or not really applicable, I urge you to go spend time with people who communicate differently to the majority of the population, it's a real eye opener.

Helping out with some sessions at the RDA gave

me opportunities to support 2 non-verbal riders. Similar in age but very different people and both highly skilled communicators.

Whilst helping out with the lesson of the first rider I was mentally preparing for the accommodations I could make for a non-verbal participant. I was planning in my head; make sure I don't ask open questions, don't talk too much, silence is fine, do ask clear questions, but don't rapid fire them and so on. How will I know if they're happy with the plans? How will I ensure we're aligned with their goals and wants? All of these plans buzzed in my head until about 90 seconds after meeting the rider.

It was clear that just because they don't verbalise does not mean they do not know exactly what they want and that they know how they're going to ask me to help them get there. It took me a further, maybe 3 minutes, to realise that they had mounted the pony, asked for stirrups to be adjusted, requested that the girth was checked, confirmed everything was now satisfactory and checked just exactly who I was without uttering a sound and being very easily understood. By the end of the lesson I realised I wasn't even consciously adjusting my planning except to make any necessary questions binary options. And the cheery disposition and ease with which they communicated makes me feel that an apt descriptor for them is "chatty"! How that makes sense when they didn't utter a word, I don't know but in my mind it truly does!

The second non-verbal rider I met sometimes utilised a speech-generating device. For everyday tasks they also were highly proficient at communicating their needs and wants with body language and simple gesture based prompts. But of course they had a lot more to say hence finding myself in a situation where the group's chairperson was running around getting buckets of water and finding us somewhere comfortable to sit. It was a baking hot day so we wanted to sit comfortably in the shade and cool our hands and feet whilst we discussed everything from the importance of on-line safety to our favourite parts of the Ashmolean Museum. I was soon looking to the rider's adult for guidance as this was no one-sided, idle chatter. The topics were sometimes challenging but how we had the conversation made it flow naturally, just slightly slower than if we were both verbalising.

Overall my take home learnings are, we aim to teach children but they somehow insist on teaching us something too. And I (and possibly much of the world) really do talk too much!

THUNDER AND LIGHTNING

by Angy Irvin

One Thursday, late summer, we (co-coach Amanda and I) spent the whole day anxiously watching the weather forecast. Was it going to thunder? Could we risk going ahead with the lesson? Should we cancel? Eventually, several ominous rumbles of thunder around half an hour before we were due to start our lesson made the decision for us. Not safe for riding – but too late to cancel the riders and helpers.

The original lesson plan had been to have gymkhana games (for the non-horsey – think sports day type races on ponies – although I haven't yet worked out how to do a sack race!!). This was revised to spending time with the ponies (assuming it wasn't actually thundering) and then some gymkhana games and steering practise on foot.

The riders duly arrived and stoically got over their disappointment that they weren't going to be riding. As it wasn't actually thundering, although the sky was very dark, they went to say hello to their pony friends and spent some time stroking noses and bonding. After a while this activity began to pall, so we went back into the indoor school and each rider chose a helper to be their "horse". (Our helpers are great and game for just about anything!!). Each rider and "horse" was given a pair of reins and the rider guided the human "horse" around – some brave helpers even closed their eyes!! Once everyone had had lots of practise we even did some gymkhana games, everyone got very competitive. The thunder didn't ever materialise but it didn't matter there was lots of laughing and making friends. Like life, RDA sessions, really are what you make of them!

THOUGHTS FROM IRIS AND THE BUNCE FAMILY

By Helen Bunce

Iris started volunteering at RDA when she was about 12, her love of horses (and indeed any animals) has always been there. It was never just about riding but their health, care and wellbeing as well. When Iris started working for the RDA this didn't change and there have been many special ponies.

When Iris broke her ankle, when she was still at school, she thought Ann would let her ride but no chance! She always told me, that if anything should happen to her I must always take her to the RDA so she could ride.

When working with animals there are hard decisions to make and losses to face. There have been many decisions like that.

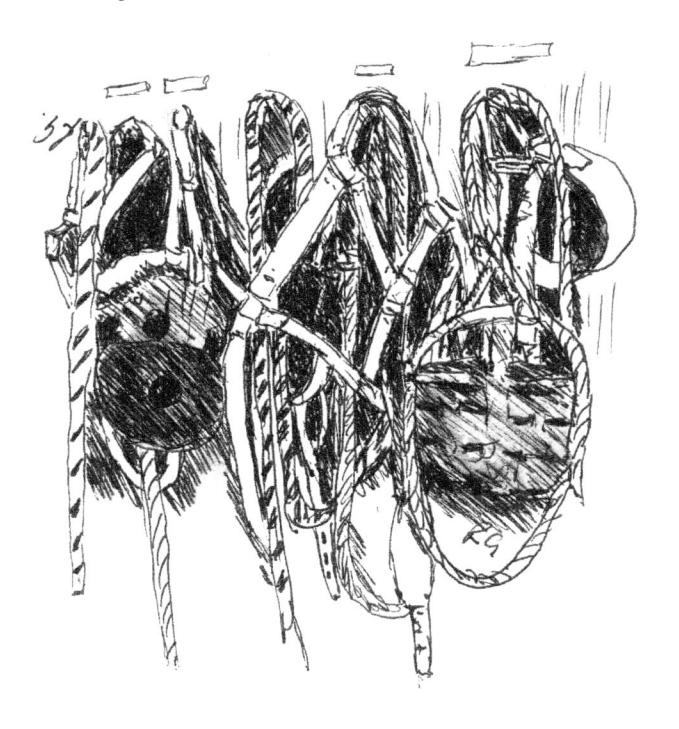

The arrival of new ponies over the years has always meant time to visit for the Bunce family.

Bryn's early days were no different. We arrived to find him running around the yard, having got out of his stable. Every time Iris got within a hand of him he was gone. He jumped over ropes, and ducked under them! 45 minutes later we managed to catch him. A few days later he was being turned out with his new friends in the fields near to the Lamb and Flag. When Iris let him go, he trotted straight across the fields, through two electric fences and into the other field. 45 minutes later we managed to retrieve him again. He chooses when he wants Iris's attention!

Iris fell in love with Ernie within days of his arrival. He would come to the fence when she arrived at the stables and whinny to her and follow her to the yard. She had always said if he was bigger he would be in her own collection of horses. His ill health recently called for a vet visit and a possible goodbye (fortunately he recovered). Whenever he sees her, he canters up and down the field and whinnies to her. He is a lovely pony with lots of character and so handsome!

We went to collect Daisy and I wasn't allowed to get out of the car as the owners were upset to let her go. So I didn't see her until we got back. This little pretty pony with loads of mane and tail, and a heart clipped into her rump, bounced out of the trailer. She trotted to the stable like a little/big dog. She had to have her mane and tail clipped for safety reasons, but still looks a little sweetie.

Time goes on - special ponies - come and go.

As will their riders.

NEARLY 50 YEARS

by Sue Taylor

I haven't quite reached 50 years of RDA
Not far off - another 5 years of going grey
I'm remembering Cox's farm next door
Enjoying horses, riders and much, much more.

Pam Gee coach, volunteers & Tesdale pupils
Weekly riding round fields with many obstacles
A steeplechaser once went much too fast
Sadly ditched his rider and went on passed.

Brave rider jumped up and managed a smile
The horse stopped promptly with cunning guile
Uneaten green grass was too much to bear
So he stuffed his face with all that was there.

Moved to Wadley with some ponies of our own
Acquired more - gosh how we had grown
There were amazing rides down to the wood
The tracks were pretty and the ponies were good

A small indoor school and we thought we were made
But with the lure of bigger and better - a seed was laid
The Lewis family offered land that we couldn't refuse
So we pulled together and begged with strategic ruse.

We made enough dosh for a brand new building
Outdoor school, fencing, gates and plenty of stabling
Tack room, kitchenette, feed room and even a loo
We moved in our horses, saddles and all the crew.

We all scrubbed up well to meet Princess Anne
Who timed her visit to perfection as royals can
She charmed us all - interested in all that we do
It all went like clockwork but how time flew.

Now we have a lovely brand new indoor school

It seems enormous and oh so very, very cool
Lots of seating, mirrors and even some jumps
We keep it all harrowed and the sand has no lumps

Now I'm feeling that I'm getting so much slower
The years gallop on and my legs lose power
As I follow grandma's trend of forgetting a name
Rider shouts "you need time out" - oh the shame!

It's wonderful to have so many new young faces
Riders progress and put ponies through paces
Thank you to all who have worked for no dime
You give our riders and horses an amazing time.

MY LOVE OF RIDING

by Seren Woollard (aged 8)

I cannot wait for a Thursday to come around each week because this is the day I get to go riding at RDA.

When I arrive at Southmoor RDA (Abingdon group) I am excited to hear which horse I am getting to ride. I particularly love to ride Maple and Rosie. Maple really interacts with me and we have a good bond. I have worked hard at RDA and can now do a great rising trot on Maple, that is my favourite part of my lesson! Rosie really listens to me when I steer my reins and when I pull them to halt.

Recently I passed my grade 1 and 2!

I enjoy telling all my friends that I get to go horse

riding every week and they all wish they could too!

MR BROWN

by Angy Irvin

If you were to picture a perfect RDA pony, you would probably picture a pony that was strong and gentle, helpful and kind who loved people. Mr Brown was the embodiment of these characteristics and he was also a little bit cheeky! Sometimes overshadowed by his awesome friend Speckles, he nevertheless spent the majority of his life at Abingdon RDA. He arrived in the early 2000s within a few years of my starting with Abingdon group. He was forgiving enough to put up with bouncy inexpert beginner trots and big and strong enough to be used with older children. He was my go to first pony for lots of medium sized beginners and a trusted pony for those coming off the lead rope for the first time. He would really try to understand what he needed to do and help his rider to do it. He soon became an old hand and would give his riders confidence.

He was definitely unflappable and became one of the few RDA ponies trained to use the hoist. (This is an invaluable contraption used to help our less mobile riders mount. The rider sits in a sling and the hoist lifts them through the air and onto the horse – as you can imagine this is fairly alarming for the horse to see their rider flying through the air and landing on them!) Over the years, Mr Brown proved a stalwart for two of my riders who mounted in this way, giving them confidence and an experience of being above the head height of their companions instead of their usual wheelchair bound restricted view of the world.

He could be cheeky and a bit greedy too. He enjoyed a richly deserved reputation as the pony that would snaffle more than the odd apple on the handy pony course whenever the opportunity arose! He also on one occasion near Easter managed to eat a whole chocolate egg – neatly removing the foil first – that was intended for his rider!

After years of service, Mr Brown, enjoyed his retirement with his friend Candy before sadly being put down in the Autumn of 2022. He is much missed. RIP Mr. Brown.

SENSATIONAL HELPERS

by Amanda Graham

I am not sure what other coaches think but I often say that my lesson lives or dies on the contribution of the helpers. And in particular some of the extra skills they bring.

I am lucky enough to have a talented primary school teacher as one of my helpers. And I have learned so much from her. Her way of communicating and eliciting good choices from the riders (and clearly her students at school) would be a great learning experience for everyone.

Here is a lovely example. A non-verbal 5 year old joined our lesson. (The non-verbal is a bit of a longer story but I will keep this fairly simple.) We decided, as we do every 18 months or so, to do proficiency tests. So we slowly introduced over the weeks the bits and pieces that they needed to learn.

We knew this rider was as bright as a button, but not only were they non-verbal, they were reticent to engage in any sort of body language. So if you said "can you point to the horse's mane?" they would (apparently) go all shy and do nothing. That is until we got to know them more, then the eyes were saying it all! However, I digress.

Here is where my great helper came in. She used a great technique which involved saying "I bet I can point to the mane before you can..." whilst she pointed to the tail or shoulder or anywhere other than the mane. It was at that point that we all had a total revelation. The rider was utterly competitive! So every time the helper did that, the rider beat her to the right answer with a big grin on her face!

When Karen came to do the "assessment" we briefed her in the competitive nature of the rider, and how she might go about it, and lo and behold they passed with flying colours.

I love my helpers!

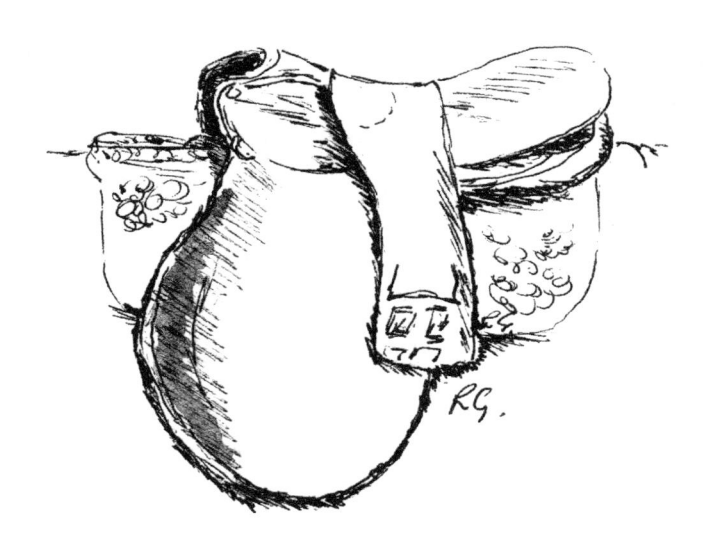

ANGY IRVIN

VOLUNTEERING

by Emily Arrowsmith

I first visited Abingdon RDA as part of a trip organised by my village Girl Guiding organisation. I was young at the time and a similar age to many of the children I currently help support at the RDA. The volunteers kindly showed me around the stables and allowed me to greet all the horses and ponies. I remember how excited I was wandering around. About 5 years later I had the pleasure of returning but as a volunteer myself. I was just as excited and 2 years later I'm still there, loving every week!

WHEN SANTA CAME TO THE PARTY...

By Angy Irvin

Often at Christmas, Abingdon RDA host a Christmas party for riders, their siblings and families. Quite often the party is held at Charney Bassett Village Hall. One year the three organisers spent a while decorating the hall in style with a Christmas tree and lots of paper snowflakes.

There were games including throw the snowball in the chimney (the snowballs weren't made of actual snow – it was far too warm – they were made from fluffy material) and dress up some of the adults as snowmen using toilet paper. This last one was great fun, the riders enjoyed wrapping me in toilet paper especially covering my face – one of the helpers had to keep rescuing me to make sure I could still breathe!! She wasn't worried about whether or not I could see (I couldn't!).

After tea a special visitor dropped in! Santa arrived! Santa sat down in a special chair with the children sitting on the floor in front of him. Santa had brought a big sack, the children all sat round expectantly as Santa explained that he had popped in to visit them and had brought them some presents. He asked who liked presents and got a show of hands (all of them I think!!). As the expectation mounted, Santa opened his sack and pulled out.... a carrot!!

"Oh no!" Santa exclaimed, "I stopped off at the stables on my way with some carrots for the ponies' Christmas presents, I must have muddled up the sacks and left them your presents!"

Santa started giving out carrots, some children were happy to accept them, then he thought again...

"I know, let's do some Santa magic and swap the sacks" he suggested. The children all said the magic words and as luck would have it the sack of presents appeared!

Santa gave out the presents to some very happy children! The ponies were happy with their carrots too!

Despite his busy schedule, before he left Santa made time for a snowball fight with the children which made for a riotous end to the party.

Thank you for visiting us Santa, we hope you come back next year...

MAKING A DIFFERENCE

by Deborah Read

My group is the first introduction to riding for many of our young RDA riders.

It is sad to say goodbye to the children at the end of their time with me but also so rewarding to see them progress forward to the next stage. Seeing them gain confidence and improvement is wonderful.

I have lots of happy memories too numerous to recite here but, there is one young teenager who I will always remember.

I was asked if I could teach a group of young boys from a local college.

Not knowing what to expect, as we were given

very little information, four apprehensive riders walked onto the gallery one Tuesday morning. Probably none of them had ever ridden or stroked a pony or a horse before.

Mickey, Luke, Jimbob and Speckles waited patiently while we mounted the riders.

It wasn't a great hit for all for them, two riders in fact tried to jump off!

After the session it was decided that just one rider would continue.

The rider in question was very shy and we were told he would not communicate with us. I put my most chatty side walker with him and by the end of the lesson he was beginning to say a little. Each week he became more confident and outgoing. His enthusiasm for riding was a joy to see and he adored Mickey.

He was quickly becoming quite a good rider and in no time he was riding without a side walker.

He also gained his Grade 1 proficiency horse care and he was so proud to receive a rosette and certificate.

Sadly, his eight weeks came to an end and despite lots of emails back and forth we were informed that he could no longer ride with us.

I can only hope he has had the opportunity to ride again as it was so beneficial for him and very rewarding for us to see him develop over such a short period of time.

I like to think that even in that brief period we made a difference for him.

VOLUNTEERING

by Nicky Warnock

They say never work with children or animals, as a teacher I know the first one is a lie, but animals?

There have been moments of complete frustration, for example, when trying to catch the little Shetland ponies to put them in their stable for the night. With the promise of his favourite nibble Marmaduke trots over to me but just as the halter reaches his ears he bolts away across the field. This happens three or four times before a more experienced volunteer steps in to help. All this is caught on camera by another volunteer and to this day I can't help but laugh at the ridiculous spectacle such a sweet tiny animal can cause.

Those same ponies were, however, charming when they met my elderly parents for 'Tea with the Ponies'.

I remember the times of trepidation when leading ponies out to the field in the dark and rain stumbling through puddles and slipping in the mud trying to remember how far it is to the gate that leads to the field called 'Lamb and Flag Near'.

But those animals seem to detect vulnerability and change character as soon as a child comes near them - they become so docile and allow hugs, tugs and tickles. They stay calm when being ridden despite any unpredictable noises or movements.

For me, volunteering at Abingdon RDA is rewarding and completely worthwhile. Getting to know the children and their families and seeing the children develop over the years. They benefit in so many ways. I watch improvements in confidence, core strength, posture and social skills - the list is endless.

I have also found it therapeutic for myself going through tough times caring for elderly parents until they sadly died last year. I'm sure my regular pony Marshall could sense when I needed a bit of comfort and as for the other volunteers ... what an amazing, dedicated, kind and supportive team!

MY RDA STORY

by Angy Irvin

As a child growing up in Worcestershire I had riding lessons at a local riding school which ran RDA sessions every Tuesday morning in term time. I remember my riding instructor talking about it and the benefits and how different our riding school ponies were with disabled riders. I always wanted to try helping but by the time I was available on Tuesday mornings (after finishing school and college) I was no longer living in the area.

Several years later, fairly newly married, I was living in an area where we knew very few people. I wanted to join something to meet people and connect with horses again so RDA seemed like the obvious choice! At the time, I had very little experience of children and virtually none of disability – it was the idea of being with horses that drew me along with meeting some like-minded people. That was back in 2001.

I was in my mid-twenties and not particularly confident. I plucked up my courage to ring up and was invited to attend on Wednesday evenings and given directions (no Satnav in those days – or if there was I didn't have it)! I arrived and was met by Gwen, who noticing my jodphurs and riding boots said "Are you my new helper? You are obviously horsey!"

This was the beginning of several years of my helping the Wednesday group. I made some friends (human and equine) and discovered the joy of making a huge difference in people's lives. I learnt a lot about life, courage in adversity and finding joy in the little things. There were some stand out ponies in those early days for me – Connor, Henry, Clipper and especially Luke. He was just about the kindest pony I have ever met.

After a spell of maternity leave, and due to childcare reasons, I returned to RDA but on a Thursday night. This offered a slightly different perspective of RDA as the riders were slightly older (mostly teenagers) and more independent both in themselves and their riding ability. After a second spell of maternity leave, I again returned to the Thursday evening group and was persuaded (I think by Gwen) to train as a coach. I was mentored by the existing coach Kate (who as I remember, wished to step down). I remember after one of my first attempts at coaching, she told me she thought being bossy came naturally to me! (She was almost certainly right!)

I qualified as a coach in 2007 and took charge of the Thursday evening class. Over the years the riders have come and gone and the single class of teenagers has morphed into two classes – one of 4-7 year olds and one of slightly older primary age riders which I run with my brilliant co-coach and friend, Amanda.

I don't know how many riders I have taught over the intervening years, but I know several of them take great delight in telling me how old they are now when I see them at events - they make me feel very old! There have been many special moments (some of which are immortalised in this and the previous book), many achievements and a few disasters. All of the riders have added to my life and I hope I have added something to theirs.

The helpers too have come and gone over the years. Many of them have turned into friends who are a big part of my life outside of RDA.

I started RDA hoping to meet people and spend time with horses, I have achieved that goal and so much more. Abingdon RDA has been the great constant in the majority of my adult life, the group has given me far more than I have given – confidence, joy, friendship, time with horses, the experience and skills to change my career - the list is endless. I may be coming up to my 24th anniversary, but I'm not going anywhere!

BRILLIANT BRYN

by Lily Mae Pearce (aged 10)

Brilliant Bryn your trot is so steady
Which is great for beginners.
The time I rode against you in a funday
You won fair and square.
When ever I go over to you after my lesson
You always come over to say hello.
You are Brillant

BRYN!

PONY TALES 2 MORE MEMORIES OF ABINGDON RDA

WHEN THE UKULELE PLAYERS CAME TO TOWN

By Amanda Graham

Late in 2024 we were approached by FADS, the Faringdon and District Strummers, who were interested in RDA Abingdon becoming their Charity Partner.

What could be better – horses and music! So we decided (amongst other things) that we would ask them to play for a drill ride for us.

Angy created a drill ride and we practised it for a few weeks. Meanwhile the group kindly appreciated that some desensitisation of the horses was needed and came along one morning to play in the big arena whilst horses Daisy, Rosie, Maple, Lisa and a few others came to meet them and listen to some songs. There were a few wild eyes to start with (the horses rather than the players!) but all went well.

So our big night arrived, freezing weather but the players arrived and we were all set. The riders and the horses were all introduced to each other and everyone warmed up. Following one practise we went for it.

They were all utterly brilliant! Horses hoof-perfect, helpers foot-perfect and riders – well riding perfectly.

We had someone taking video, the large arena lends itself to wonderful photographs with the big mirror behind.

As part of the practise the leader of the group, worked out the perfect timing to end the drill ride with Eric Clapton's song – Wonderful Tonight. Think of those lines "my darling, you are wonderful tonight" and you will get a sense of how emotional it was.

I will end this story with a couple of messages from the helpers…

"I had a bit of an emotional moment with the music and leading the horses !!! It must be my age xxx"

"I'm with you…felt super emotional watching the video!
It looks amazing!!!
Well done."

MY LIFE WITH RDA - SO FAR!

By Victoria Griffiths

It is both the 55th Anniversary of RDA and the 50th Anniversary of Abingdon RDA next year. A good time to look back and reflect.

I was fortunate to share 2 ponies with my sister and two brothers. We didn't have lessons or smart clothes, and the ponies were super scruffy. We did hack to the odd Pony Club rally or competition and loved to join the Boxing Day hunt that always started from our village 'common'. But we also hacked to an indoor school several miles away on a Sunday afternoon to be part of Gaddeston Place RDA Group. The format was a million miles away from the professional organisation we now have (and what they now have) – pony owners would turn up, riders would turn up and there would be some circuits round the school. Lots of laughing when struggling to mount the riders and lots of fun in general. I'm not sure we even bothered with hats! This was in 1975, 50 years ago, the same year Abingdon started.

We then moved to West Wales and my mother set up an RDA Group there. My really naughty 14.2 Chestnut cob called Brandy could deposit any 'good' rider on the floor with Pony Club instructors his speciality, but he was chosen to be presented to Princess Anne as the best RDA pony in the region. He was absolutely bomb proof with an RDA rider and much loved.

Fast forward to 1998, married with kids and living near Abingdon. I had just bought a first pony (12h Palomino mare called Amber) for my daughter who had asked every day for a year! A lady called Mary living in the village accosted me one day and said I should help at Abingdon RDA – any of you who remember Mary will know that saying 'no' was not an option. A carload of us would leave Drayton Post Office at ten past nine every Wednesday to help Sue Taylor with the Kingfisher class.

That was 26 years ago, and I am still helping Sue with the Kingfisher Class. We are the only 2 remaining from that time although Clare, the member of staff who brings the children, is still the same. A treasure and so committed to the experience we provide for the children.

Over the years, there have been many close shaves with riders 'bailing out', removing clothing, refusing hats, mounting, dismounting, with saddles slipping round, bucks, shies and bolts but the positives far outweigh them all. Hearing a non-verbal child say 'walk on', watching the smiles and seeing the progress from flat out refusal to laughing with delight keep our Wednesday team motivated and committed.

I have progressed from 'helping' to being a coach myself and though my favourite class will always be Kingfisher with Sue, I do learn so much from my other classes, be they teenagers, adults or tinies. Talking of favourites; the summer Ridgeway rides organised by Milla have provided some very special memories. Speckles was my first of many 'able bodied first day' rides but it was the transformation in both the ponies and riders that surprised me most each year. They loved the change of scene and rose to the challenge.

To my husband's horror (!), once I retired, I became a Trustee and Group Treasurer – this has opened my eyes to the enormous amount of effort and time it takes to run this group.

As a footnote, my mother maintained her connection to RDA continuing to run groups well into her 80s. A tough act to follow.

A ROYAL VISIT

by Melanie Charles

I started volunteering at Abingdon RDA when I was 17 years old and wondering what to do in my summer holiday. At that time we were based just outside Faringdon, had a tiny little school and fewer ponies. (But we did have lovely access straight onto a bridle way!) The tack room was a converted stable and there was a caravan where volunteers could shelter! Plans were afoot to move the group and after an awful lot of wheeling, dealing, negotiating and fund raising that took years, we moved the whole yard to the current site and to the purpose built indoor school and stalls.

Such splendid new surroundings needed a special opening ceremony and we were lucky enough to have Her Royal Highness The Princess Royal come and open it for us. By this time I was teaching at a school in Abingdon and coaching on a Tuesday evening and volunteering during the school holidays. This is back in the day when becoming a coach was as easy as Ann Barlow saying "Come on, you can do that!" And no one can every say no to Ann.....

The great day arrived, and every class had organised a part of the display for Her Royal Highness. We were all briefed that she would not talk to the coaches or volunteers as all her focus would be on the riders. This was certainly true. The Princess watched the more than 100 riders with such attention that, as she gave them their rosettes, she chatted to them about their riding, talked to them about how their pony had gone and gave them tips on how to improve. She was absolutely amazing.

Because I knew all the ponies and had worked with a lot of the riders, I ended up leading ponies in 3 different parts of the display. On the third occasion The Princess Royal surprised me by talking to me. She said "You have had a really busy morning! Will I be seeing you again?" and we had a quick chat about the pony I was leading. It was an unforgettable morning made very special by Her

Royal Highness and her dedication to making it special for all.

THE NEW ARENA

by Ann Barlow

Thinking back over this massive project, one of my abiding memories is the extraordinary people who were able to cope with someone who had taken on a huge task with no idea of what was to come over the next 6 years. I had no knowledge of anything to do with building, let alone agricultural building, but without exception, every one of the experts that stepped in, were wonderful, and helped me to understand what was going on, what was next, and what was to follow. I cannot thank them all enough.

The first pitfall was planning, but thanks to Adrian and his team it all went smoothly, and permission was granted on 27th March 2015. The next step was painful – fundraising for a vast amount of money, and this basically took 4 years. Planning permission only lasts for 3 years, so in 2018 we had to start work. Gordon and his grandsons took on the huge task of laying the groundwork – I learnt a great deal about bolts and sub base specifications! COVID then intervened and work had to stop, but the weeds had a ball! On the 15th February 2021 Bill from Shufflebottoms and his team arrived, and by the evening of the 18th the steel building frame was up – they were delightful to work with and never disturbed the day to day running of the yard.

Electricity was next followed by kick boards and the laying of the surface, and then we were on our way to the finished product, and the arena was opened on the 11th September 2021 by Ed Brasher, the National Office CEO., who cut the ribbon, whereupon the flood gates opened, and the hordes descended! This was followed by an incredible tribute to Abingdon RDA by Ed.

To raise this enormous amount of money was daunting, but with the help of members of RDA, the public and very large grants from Trusts and Foundations, we somehow made it to the final figure of about £270,000!! This huge sum raised was solely restricted money for this project.

I think many thought this could never happen, and it would never have happened had it not been for the amazing support given to me by wonderful groups of people, and particularly Sally, who helped and supported me all the way.

As someone put it to me "This great plan to build a mythical structure would require a lot of tombolas!!"

After the horrors of COVID this massive building was a huge lift for the Group, and this new facility has brought endless new opportunities for our disabled riders and has been a great joy to horsey members of the public, many of whom hire the school on a regular basis. We hold training days, competitions and regular fundraising events in the arena, all of which are enjoyed by many.

This was a huge undertaking but we are all absolutely thrilled with the end result and as I said before a huge thank you goes to Adrian who sorted planning permission, Gordon and his grandsons who laid the groundwork, Rosemary and Bill from Shufflebottoms, Mark from O&O Electricals, Colin who fixed the kickboards and Colin from Andrews Bowen who laid the surface.

ALESSIA'S STORY

by Chantal Lewis

Alessia started at RDA Abingdon after being referred by her physio Suzie to help with independent sitting. She was around 2 years old and could not sit independently, so she was able to have 4 x 15 minute sessions riding bareback with a lovely physio on a big shire cross horse called Mickey. Alessia wasn't terribly keen but the physio was very kind and continued with gentle exercises on Mickey who was the ultimate professional therapy horse. I couldn't believe the huge progress after only 4 sessions, Alessia was very soon sitting independently. I do remember one of the sessions when one of the helpers who was leading Mickey and wasn't paying full attention, bless Mickey he stepped on her foot by accident.......big ouch!!!! A clear lesson to me to ensure I keep my feet away from hooves.

I was then keen to get Alessia to have more

therapeutic riding with RDA Abingdon. We went on the waiting list and struck lucky and was given a space on a Tuesday morning, Deborah's group lesson. Alessia rode Star, a lovely small grey pony who had great experience and tolerance. Alessia again wasn't terribly keen as she was actually having to work quite hard, she cried and wanted to get off. Sessions were just a few minutes, 5 minutes and then gradually a little longer each time. I thought we would have to give up but on the fourth session she didn't cry, phew!

Charlie was the next pony she rode, another small grey pony who was bomb proof, but was swift when he wanted to be, ha ha!

Alessia grew stronger and stronger, her core muscles developing all the time until she did eventually start to walk which is hugely challenging due to her hypotonia, it's hard work! When Alessia has been poorly and missed her riding sessions her walking ability is significantly reduced, the wonderful ponies at RDA Abingdon truly ensure Alessia continues to be ambulant.

Other ponies Alessia has ridden are the gentle ex gypsy pony Meg, who had a lovely rhythmic plod. Mr Brown was a big favourite, he was such a good boy tolerating Alessia flapping about and making funny noises sometimes. We'd sneakily give him a polo mint sometimes, sssshhh don't tell Ann, hee hee.

Fundays in September have always been fun, everybody mucking in, prepping ponies, wonderful food, drink and cake. Alessia has dressed up a few times to ride on the day, as a ladybird and fairy, a couple of the outfits which the ponies were happy to parade.

All the staff and volunteers work so hard to enable all the children and adults to ride, we are so massively grateful (they even sing to Alessia when she requests it), Alessia's riding session each week is a huge highlight for her. Massive thank you to all.

BRYN'S SORE TEETH

by Amanda Graham

Amanda: Hello Bryn how are you?
Bryn: Hello Amanda I'm fine thank you
Amanda: Are you ready to come and help your rider have some fun?
Bryn: Yes please!
Bryn: Oh no, no, no you're going to hurt me
Amanda: Oh Bryn we won't I promise
Bryn: But my teeth are so sore
Amanda: Angy is coming and she is your special person, you remember she is really gentle.
Amanda: Can I come in your stall?
Bryn: Yes
Amanda: Shall we just chill a while?
Bryn: Yes we can watch Lisa
Amanda: What is Lisa doing?
Bryn: She's telling me that all the herd is together and watching out for each other
Amanda: What is she watching out for?

Bryn: The lion

Amanda: The lion?

Bryn: Yes the one that lives in the trees, doesn't come out often but when I catch a movement in the side of my eye I get very frightened he will come and eat me.

Amanda: Gosh Bryn, we will make sure he doesn't get you, and as you say, the herd will tell you if something is wrong. Ah here's Angy

Angy: Hello Bryn

Bryn: Hello Angy

Angy: Are you ready to give your rider a fantastic and fun ride?

Bryn: I always do

Angy: Yes you do Bryn

Amanda: Can I make you feel a bit more comfortable by putting your reins around your neck?

Bryn: No, no, no

Amanda: I promise Bryn, Angy won't hurt your teeth

Bryn: OK then

Angy: Can I put your bridle on? Have it here in my hand, look.

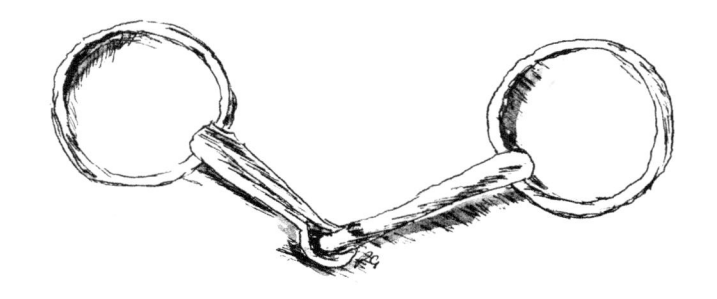

Bryn: No no no

Bryn: Ok I'll just hold it close to you for a while then we'll do it really slowly and gently and not clunk your teeth

Amanda: Who is your best friend on the yard Bryn?

Bryn: Why Jim Bob of course!

Amanda: Because?

Bryn: We like to groom each other and eat grass together and chase around the field having fun, and sometimes fisty cuffs! Then when Iris comes we go and say hello then run away again for a game.

Angy: There you go Bryn all done, such a good boy

Bryn: My bridle's on?

Angy: Yep!

Bryn, Angy, Amanda: Let's go and have fun!

ANGY IRVIN

MY DRAWING OF BRYN

By Willow Frith (age 5)

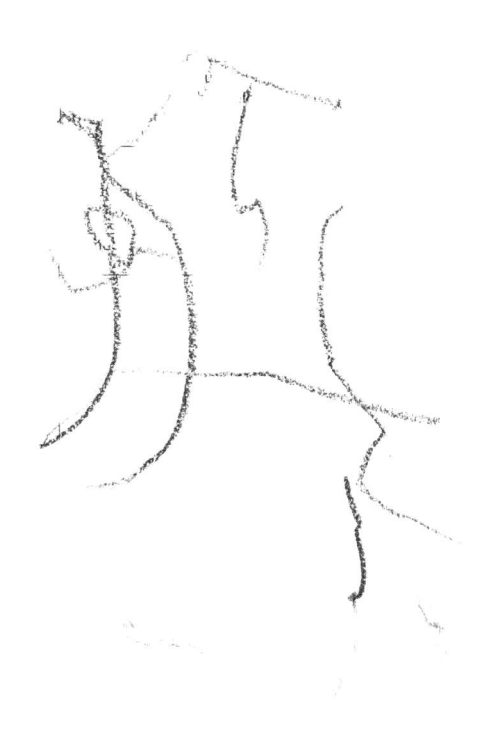

THANK YOU

Thank you to all the horses who have been part of Abingdon RDA. I have tried to list them all below along with a few words to remember them by. If you can remember any others please let me know.

AJ	Bouncy, off you go!
Arthur	Big
Bilbo	So adorable that the Lady of Wadley Manor wanted to buy him.
Bill	Big, steady, grey.
Blue	Chubby little grey
Bob	Cute, little dynamo
Bobby	Fast with a mind of his own!
Boots	Inseparable with Chrissy
Boris	A great character who snuck into a few wedding pics!
Bouncer	Quiet enough for little ones to "hike" lying down
Boysey	Ready to give his all
Brandy	Brilliant at dressage
Bryn	A bit of an escape artist!
Callum	A lovely ride
Camden	
Candy	As sweet as her name, if she liked you
Casper	A bit of a challenge!
Charlie	A cheeky little chap!
Charlie B	Enjoyed dressage
Chase	An ocean liner!

PONY TALES 2 MORE MEMORIES OF ABINGDON RDA

Chrissy	Inseparable from Boots
Clipper	Affectionately known as "ClipClop"
Conner	Irish Gent
Daisy	Popular on Facebook!
Dandy	A fine and dandy character!
Dasher	Not that well named! Walk was his preferred pace!
Deliah	A lovely grey, but not fond of RDA work so didn't stay long!
Dipper	
Dobin	A lovely grey driving horse
Drago	The steadiest and widest of backs
Duchess	Large and stately baby
Duke	A true gentleman
Elbow	Knows her own mind
Ernie	Handsome chap
Ettie	A mini race horse
Flipper	A blast from the past - very popular

◆ ◆ ◆

Fly	
Fred (new)	Steady with a few tricks up his sleeve.
Freddie	Led Marmaduke astray (or the other way around)
Garva	A much loved Connemara
George	A wise, kind head on young shoulders
Harlequin	Suspect brakes!
Harry	Cracking little pony who loves RDA
Hector	Brakes sometimes needed attention!
Henry	Gwen's boy
Hope	A mare with mare tendencies in abundance
Hugo	Dark coloured coblet
Jasper	Epitome of a Thelwell pony
JayJay	A sweetie!
JB	A marmite horse
Jock	A strong Haflinger who could jump out of his stall!
John	Big skewbald
Leo	Very big, beautiful chestnut

ANGY IRVIN

Lisa	The loveliest of ladies
Lisa (2)	"She listens to what I tell her"
Luke	The kindest horse I have ever met
Magic	Lived to 39, enjoying retirement with Sue T.
Malcolm	Ernie's best mate
Maple	A go ahead girl
Marmaduke	Led Freddie astray (or the other way around!)
Marshall	The most trustworthy of ponies
May	A steady darling girl
Meg	A kind, generous girl
Merlin	Purchased from a trekking centre - needed a lot of leg!
Mickey	A Gentle Giant!
Minstrel	Amazing pony
Mouse	Inquisitive and in your face (in a nice way!)
Mr Brown	Rock steady RDA pony (mostly!)
Noah	Handsome dark grey

◆ ◆ ◆

Nooky Bear	Always did the best he could for every rider
Pi	Stunning
Piglet	Didn't grow into a pig
Plum	Lovely steady girl
Polly	Little, chestnut beauty
Polo	Loved gymkhana and understood "Go!"
Prin (Princess)	Survived an RTC on the way to RDA
Raddish	Loved to surprise - when she was good she was very very good...
Ranger	Not so fond of the pond
Rocky	Well loved grey
Rondo	Ever the gentleman, the best RDA horse
Rooster	Full of explosive fun
Rosie	As sweet as a rosebud
Rosie (2)	Beautiful Lady
Roxy	Not always great to load!
Sammy	More beauty than brains

PONY TALES 2 MORE MEMORIES OF ABINGDON RDA

Shannon	
Simba	Heart of a lion
Sophie	Sweet and always cheerful, great gymkhana pony
Speckles	A true legend - a perfect RDA pony
Star	Well-named!
Trilly	Lovely, but could kick!
Tufty	A kind and clever friend
Warrior	Black pony with a great temperament
Weggs	A bit on the wild side
William	Enjoyed civil war re-enactment
Wizard	A magic pony
Yorkie	A sweet little boy!

ACKNOWLEDGEMENT

Thank you to all the contributors:

Emily Arrowsmith
Ann Barlow
Katherine Brimblecombe
Helen Bunce
Alex Busby
Nikki Busby
Caitlin Cartledge
Michael Cartledge
Bella Chandler
Melanie Charles
Lesley Chaundy
Sam Davies
Alina Maria Dina
Lorrie Dinger
Hazel Frith
Willow Frith
Amanda Graham
Isaac Grange

Sarah Heyburn
Chloe Humphries
Victoria Griffiths
Angy Irvin
Chantal Lewis
Helene James-Menard
Megs Marriott
Sue Murrin
Tilly O'Shea
Jenny & Rob Pace
Lily Mae Pearce
Deborah Read
Jo Sproston
Tim Stimpson
Karen Stubbs
Sue Taylor
Lyndsey Trickett
Nicky Warnock
Seren Woollard

The photographers:

Amanda Graham
Ian Graham
Angy Irvin
Sarah Cantlay

and to the following for their invaluable assistance:

Ann Barlow

Lesley Chaundy
Amanda Graham
Ian Graham
Victoria Griffiths
Karen Stubbs
Sue Taylor

and special thanks to Ruth Gerring for her wonderful ink drawings and Val Evans for her amazing cover design.

Printed in Great Britain
by Amazon